**POWER
POSITIVITY**

I AM
STRONG

Hardie Grant

BOOKS

MY COURAGE ALWAYS RISES AT EVERY ATTEMPT TO INTIMIDATE ME.

Jane Austen, *Pride and Prejudice*

I BELIEVE IT'S TIME THAT WOMEN TRULY OWNED THEIR SUPERPOWERS AND USED THEIR BEAUTY AND STRENGTH TO CHANGE THE WORLD AROUND THEM.

Janelle Monáe

I FOUND STRENGTH IN WHAT HURT ME. AND IN MY FAMILY – THAT'S MY STRENGTH AS WELL. I'M TRULY GRATEFUL TO BE HURT AS MANY TIMES AS I HAVE BECAUSE I'M HAPPY.

Selena Gomez

YOUR VULNERABILITY IS WHERE YOUR REAL STRENGTH LIES.

Oprah Winfrey

STRENGTH DOES NOT COME FROM WINNING. YOUR STRUGGLES DEVELOP YOUR STRENGTHS.

Arnold Schwarzenegger

FAILURE GAVE ME STRENGTH. PAIN WAS MY MOTIVATION.

Michael Jordan

THE TERRORISTS THOUGHT
THEY WOULD CHANGE MY
AIMS AND STOP MY AMBITIONS,
BUT NOTHING CHANGED IN MY
LIFE EXCEPT THIS: WEAKNESS,
FEAR AND HOPELESSNESS
DIED. STRENGTH, POWER
AND COURAGE WERE BORN.

Malala Yousafzai

I REALISED THAT IF I DON'T
LIKE SOMETHING, I CAN
CHANGE IT. IF I DON'T
FEEL COMFORTABLE WITH
SOMETHING, THEN I HAVE A
VOICE TO SAY IT'S NOT COOL.

Zendaya

THE DISTANCE IS NOTHING; IT IS ONLY THE FIRST STEP THAT IS DIFFICULT.

Madame du Deffand

YOU DO NOT HAVE TO BE FEARLESS; JUST DON'T LET FEAR STOP YOU.

Charlie Day

YOU WERE GIVEN THIS LIFE BECAUSE YOU ARE STRONG ENOUGH TO LIVE IT.

WHENEVER YOU FIND YOURSELF DOUBTING HOW FAR YOU CAN GO, JUST REMEMBER HOW FAR YOU HAVE COME.

HAVING EMOTIONS
DOES NOT MAKE YOU
WEAK. EVEN FEAR
AND ANGER CAN
BE USED TO DRIVE
YOU FORWARD.

YOU'RE ALLOWED TO SCREAM, YOU'RE ALLOWED TO CRY, BUT DO NOT GIVE UP.

SOMETIMES YOU FACE DIFFICULTIES NOT BECAUSE YOU'RE DOING SOMETHING WRONG, BUT BECAUSE YOU'RE DOING SOMETHING RIGHT.

WORK YOUR BUTT OFF. YOU NEVER WANT TO FAIL BECAUSE YOU DIDN'T WORK HARD ENOUGH.

Arnold Schwarzenegger

I SEE MYSELF AS A SURVIVOR
AND I'M NOT ASHAMED TO
SAY I'M A SURVIVOR. TO ME,
A SURVIVOR IMPLIES STRENGTH,
IMPLIES THAT I HAVE BEEN
THROUGH SOMETHING, AND
I MADE IT OUT THE OTHER SIDE.

Elizabeth Smart

LIFE SHRINKS OR EXPANDS IN PROPORTION TO ONE'S COURAGE.

Anaïs Nin

THE STRONGEST THING A WOMAN CAN DO IS TO LOVE HERSELF AND BE HERSELF.

A STRONG WOMAN
IS ONE WHO IS ABLE
TO SMILE IN THE MORNING
LIKE SHE WASN'T
CRYING LAST NIGHT.

THE STRONGEST PEOPLE ARE NOT THOSE WHO SHOW STRENGTH IN FRONT OF US BUT THOSE WHO FIGHT BATTLES WE KNOW NOTHING ABOUT.

SOMETIMES YOU HAVE TO GET KNOCKED DOWN LOWER THAN YOU HAVE EVER BEEN TO STAND TALLER THAN YOU EVER WERE.

SMILE AND LET
EVERYONE KNOW
THAT TODAY YOU'RE
A LOT STRONGER
THAN YOU WERE
YESTERDAY.

THE STRUGGLE YOU'RE IN TODAY IS DEVELOPING THE STRENGTH YOU NEED FOR TOMORROW.

YOU CAN BECOME STRONG AND POWERFUL AND BEAUTIFUL.

Serena Williams

NEVER BE ASHAMED OF A SCAR. IT SIMPLY MEANS YOU WERE STRONGER THAN WHATEVER TRIED TO HURT YOU.

I KNOW WHO I AM
AND I KNOW WHO
I'M NOT. I KNOW MY
SHORTCOMINGS,
I KNOW MY STRENGTHS;
MAYBE SOME OF
MY SHORTCOMINGS
ARE MY STRENGTHS.

Mark Ruffalo

**THIS IS THE YEAR
I WILL BE STRONGER,
BRAVER, KINDER,
UNSTOPPABLE.**

STORMS MAKE TREES TAKE DEEPER ROOTS.

Dolly Parton

IF SOMETHING'S NOT A CHALLENGE, THERE'S NO POINT DOING IT BECAUSE YOU'RE NOT GONNA LEARN MUCH.

Tom Holland

YOU ARE STRONGER THAN YOU THINK.

**GO AS FAR AS YOU THINK
YOU CAN AND THEN
TAKE ANOTHER STEP.**

BE THE HEROINE OF YOUR LIFE, NOT THE VICTIM.

Nora Ephron

**COURAGE IS THE PRICE
THAT LIFE EXACTS
FOR GRANTING PEACE.**

Amelia Earhart

LOVE IS LIFE; FEAR IS NOT AN OPTION.

Diane von Furstenberg

**WHAT WOULD
YOU DO IF YOU
WEREN'T AFRAID?**

THERE IS STRENGTH INSIDE YOU THAT YOU DON'T YET KNOW.

BEING BOTH SOFT AND STRONG IS A COMBINATION VERY FEW HAVE MASTERED.

IF YOU NEVER HAD TO STRUGGLE, YOU'D NEVER GROW STRONGER.

YOU CAN AND YOU WILL.

YOU HAVE TO BE AT YOUR STRONGEST WHEN YOU'RE FEELING YOUR WEAKEST.

IT'S OKAY TO
BE SCARED.
BEING SCARED MEANS
YOU'RE DOING
SOMETHING BRAVE.

MY SOLE STRENGTH IS IN MY TENACITY.

Louis Pasteur

ANYTHING'S POSSIBLE.
IF I TURN AROUND TOMORROW
AND SAY I WANT TO BE
A SPACEMAN, I COULD DO
THAT. YOU CAN DO WHATEVER
YOU WANT TO DO.

Sam Smith

AS HARD AS IT IS, OWNING
WHO YOU ARE AND KNOWING
WHAT YOU WANT IS THE ONLY
SURE PATH TO AFFIRMATION ...
I WANT WOMEN TO KNOW
THEY CAN GET OUT OF ANY
SITUATION IF THEY RETURN
TO THEIR CORE SOURCE OF
STRENGTH: THEMSELVES.

Ashley Graham

COURAGE IS RESISTANCE TO FEAR, MASTERY OF FEAR – NOT ABSENCE OF FEAR.

Mark Twain

**ANYONE CAN GIVE UP.
IT'S THE EASIEST THING
IN THE WORLD TO DO.
BUT TO KEEP GOING AFTER
A FAILURE IS TRUE STRENGTH.**

YOU NEVER REALISE HOW STRONG YOU ARE ...

UNTIL BEING STRONG IS THE ONLY CHOICE YOU HAVE.

A STRONG WOMAN
STANDS UP FOR
HERSELF. A STRONGER
WOMAN STANDS UP
FOR EVERYONE ELSE.

IF YOU DOUBT YOUR POWER, YOU GIVE POWER TO YOUR DOUBTS.

STAY STRONG. MAKE THEM WONDER HOW YOU'RE STILL SMILING.

**KITES RISE
HIGHEST AGAINST
THE WIND.**

**PEOPLE ARE LIKE
TEA BAGS – THEY
DON'T KNOW THEIR
OWN STRENGTH
UNTIL THEY GET
INTO HOT WATER.**

I'VE NEVER MET A WOMAN WHO IS NOT STRONG, BUT SOMETIMES THEY DON'T LET IT OUT. THEN THERE'S A TRAGEDY AND THEN ALL OF A SUDDEN THAT STRENGTH COMES. MY MESSAGE IS LET THE STRENGTH COME OUT BEFORE THE TRAGEDY.

Diane von Furstenberg

TINA TURNER IS SOMEONE THAT I ADMIRE BECAUSE SHE MADE HER STRENGTH FEMININE AND SEXY.

Beyoncé

I DON'T WANT OTHER PEOPLE TO DECIDE WHO I AM. I WANT TO DECIDE THAT FOR MYSELF.

Emma Watson

**BE SURE YOU
PUT YOUR FEET IN
THE RIGHT PLACE,
THEN STAND FIRM.**

Abraham Lincoln

STRENGTH DOES NOT COME FROM PHYSICAL CAPACITY. IT COMES FROM AN INDOMITABLE WILL.

Mahatma Gandhi

WITH THE NEW DAY COMES NEW STRENGTH AND NEW THOUGHTS.

Eleanor Roosevelt

SOMETIMES THOSE MISTAKES LEAD YOU TO YOUR EXACT PURPOSE AND WHAT YOU'RE SUPPOSED TO BE.

Jennifer Lopez

WHEN YOU FEEL STRONG, USE THAT STRENGTH TO HELP THOSE WHO ARE WEAK.

PERFECT COURAGE IS TO DO WITHOUT WITNESSES WHAT ONE WOULD BE CAPABLE OF DOING WITH THE WORLD LOOKING ON.

François de La Rochefoucauld

STRENGTH DOESN'T MEAN NEVER GIVING UP. IT MEANS NEVER GIVING UP ON YOURSELF.

NEVER SILENCE YOURSELF
OUT OF FEAR THAT THE
TRUTH YOU SPEAK MIGHT
PROVOKE; BE COURAGEOUS.

Chimamanda
Ngozie Adichie

COURAGE IS THE MOST IMPORTANT OF ALL THE VIRTUES, BECAUSE WITHOUT COURAGE YOU CAN'T PRACTICE ANY OTHER VIRTUES CONSISTENTLY.

Maya Angelou

**ALL OUR DREAMS CAN
COME TRUE IF WE HAVE THE
COURAGE TO PURSUE THEM.**

Walt Disney

MOST OF THE IMPORTANT THINGS IN THE WORLD HAVE BEEN ACCOMPLISHED BY PEOPLE WHO HAVE KEPT ON TRYING WHEN THERE SEEMED TO BE NO HOPE AT ALL.

Dale Carnegie

YOUR COURAGE IS LIKE A MUSCLE. YOU HAVE TO USE IT TO MAKE IT STRONGER.

THAT WHICH DOES NOT KILL US MAKES US STRONGER.

Friedrich Nietzsche

THERE IS NOBODY WHO'S SUCCESSFUL WHO HAS NEVER THOUGHT ABOUT QUITTING ... IT'S POWERING THROUGH THOSE TIMES WHEN YOU FEEL LIKE YOU CAN'T MAKE IT.

LL Cool J

HAVING THE STRENGTH TO TUNE OUT NEGATIVITY AND REMAIN FOCUSED ON WHAT I WANT GIVES ME THE WILL AND CONFIDENCE TO ACHIEVE MY GOALS.

Gisele Bundchen

I'M VERY TINY AND I AM VERY
EMOTIONAL, AND THAT IS NOT
SOMETHING PEOPLE USUALLY
ASSOCIATE WITH STRENGTH.
I THINK WEAKNESS, IN A WAY,
CAN BE ALSO NEEDED BECAUSE
WE DON'T HAVE TO BE THE
LOUDEST, WE DON'T HAVE TO TAKE
UP THE MOST AMOUNT OF SPACE,
AND WE DON'T HAVE TO EARN
THE MOST MONEY ... WE NEED TO
CARE ABOUT EACH OTHER MORE.

Greta Thunberg

SCARS ARE LIKE BATTLE
WOUNDS – BEAUTIFUL IN
A WAY. THEY SHOW WHAT
YOU'VE BEEN THROUGH
AND HOW STRONG YOU
ARE FOR COMING OUT OF IT.

Demi Lovato

WHAT GETS YOU THROUGH LIFE IS STRENGTH OF CHARACTER AND STRENGTH OF SPIRIT AND LOVE.

Viola Davis

YOU'VE BEEN HURT
BEFORE, AND YOU
SURVIVED. YOU
CAN DO IT AGAIN.

THE WAY I DRESS AND
CARRY MYSELF, A LOT OF
PEOPLE FIND IT INTIMIDATING.
I THINK MY WHOLE CAREER
CAN BE BOILED DOWN TO
THE ONE WORD I ALWAYS
SAY IN MEETINGS: STRENGTH.

Lorde

WHAT GIVES ME STRENGTH
ALL THE TIME IS TO BE ABLE TO
HAVE FORMULATED A GROUP
OF PEOPLE AROUND ME THAT
ARE MY FRIENDS AND MY
FAMILY – THOSE TWO WORDS
ARE ENMESHED IN MY OPINION –
IT'S GIVEN ME A GROUNDING.

Leonardo di Caprio

I THINK MY LOT IN LIFE IS
TO BATTLE. I DON'T MEAN IT
LIKE YOU'RE ALWAYS TENSE
AND FIGHTING. IT'S THE LONG
BATTLE, SOMETHING YOU
DON'T WIN WITH MUSCULAR
STRENGTH. YOU WIN IT
WITH MENTAL FORTITUDE.

Joan Jett

I'M NOT AFRAID. LIFE IS JUST SUCH AN ADVENTURE TO ME.

Elizabeth Taylor

BEING GLAMOUROUS IS ABOUT STRENGTH AND CONFIDENCE.

Catherine Zeta-Jones

**IT'S NEVER TOO
LATE TO RECLAIM
YOUR INNER DIVA
AND RECLAIM YOUR
INNER STRENGTH.**

Michelle Visage

I DO BELIEVE IN THE OLD SAYING 'WHAT DOES NOT KILL YOU MAKES YOU STRONGER.' OUR EXPERIENCES, GOOD AND BAD, MAKE US WHO WE ARE. BY OVERCOMING DIFFICULTIES, WE GAIN STRENGTH AND MATURITY.

Angelina Jolie

I AM AN EXAMPLE OF WHAT
IS POSSIBLE WHEN GIRLS
FROM THE VERY BEGINNING OF
THEIR LIVES ARE LOVED AND
NURTURED BY PEOPLE AROUND
THEM. I WAS SURROUNDED BY
EXTRAORDINARY WOMEN IN MY
LIFE WHO TAUGHT ME ABOUT
QUIET STRENGTH AND DIGNITY.

Michelle Obama

I REALISED THAT MY STRENGTH WAS BEING DIFFERENT.

Betsey Johnson

MY INNER STRENGTH
COMES FROM MY
FRIENDS. I HAVE
A VERY CLOSE
GROUP OF FRIENDS
AND FAMILY AND
WE ALL HELP EACH
OTHER THROUGH
OUR DARK TIMES.

Kathy Bates

I ALLOW MYSELF TO FAIL. I ALLOW MYSELF TO BREAK. I'M NOT AFRAID OF MY FLAWS.

Lady Gaga

THE STRENGTH OF THE PACK IS THE WOLF, AND THE STRENGTH OF THE WOLF IS THE PACK.

Rudyard Kipling

I AM STRONG BECAUSE I'VE BEEN WEAK.

**THERE'S BOLDNESS
IN BEING ASSERTIVE
AND THERE'S STRENGTH
AND CONFIDENCE.**

Bryan Cranston

YOU DON'T KNOW HOW MANY
TIMES PEOPLE HAVE TOLD ME
THAT THEY'D BEEN DOWN AND
DEPRESSED AND JUST WANTED
TO DIE. BUT THEN A SPECIAL
SONG CAUGHT THEIR EAR
AND THAT HELPED GIVE THEM
RENEWED STRENGTH. THAT'S
THE POWER MUSIC HAS.

Mary J Blige

WE LIVE IN A WORLD WHERE
TO ADMIT ANYTHING NEGATIVE
ABOUT YOURSELF IS SEEN
AS A WEAKNESS, WHEN IT'S
ACTUALLY A STRENGTH. IT'S
NOT A WEAK MOVE TO SAY
'I NEED HELP.'

Jon Hamm

Published in 2022 by
Hardie Grant Books, an imprint
of Hardie Grant Publishing

Hardie Grant Books (London)
5th & 6th Floors
52–54 Southwark Street
London SE1 1UN

Hardie Grant Books (Melbourne)
Building 1, 658 Church Street
Richmond, Victoria 3121

hardiegrantbooks.com

British Library Cataloguing-in-
Publication Data. A catalogue
record for this book is available
from the British Library.

I AM STRONG
by Hardie Grant Books

ISBN: 9781784885328

Publishing Director: Kajal Mistry
Acting Publishing Director:
Emma Hopkin
Commissioning Editor: Kate Burkett
Text curated by: Satu Fox
Editorial Assistant: Harriet Thornley
Design: Claire Warner Studio

Colour Reproduction by p2d
Printed and bound in China by
Leo Paper Products Ltd.

MIX
Paper from
responsible sources
FSC™ C020056
www.fsc.org